Cute Cat
Coloring Book

CREATIVE COLORING PRESS

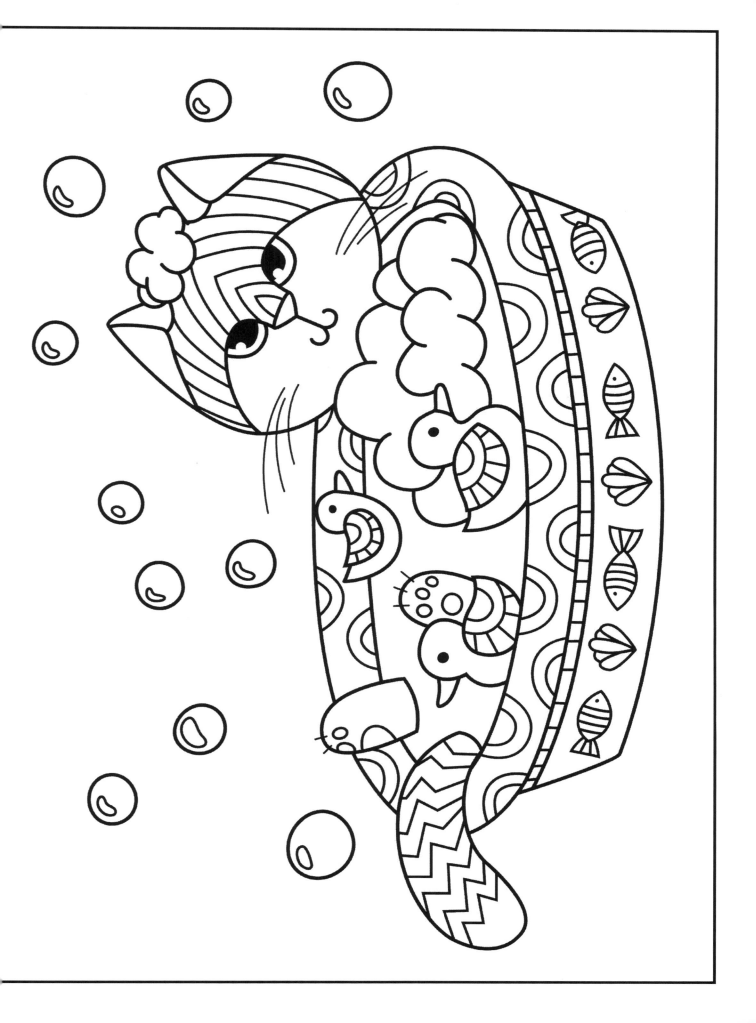

Bonus Pages

Turn the page for bonus pages from some of our most popular coloring and activity books.

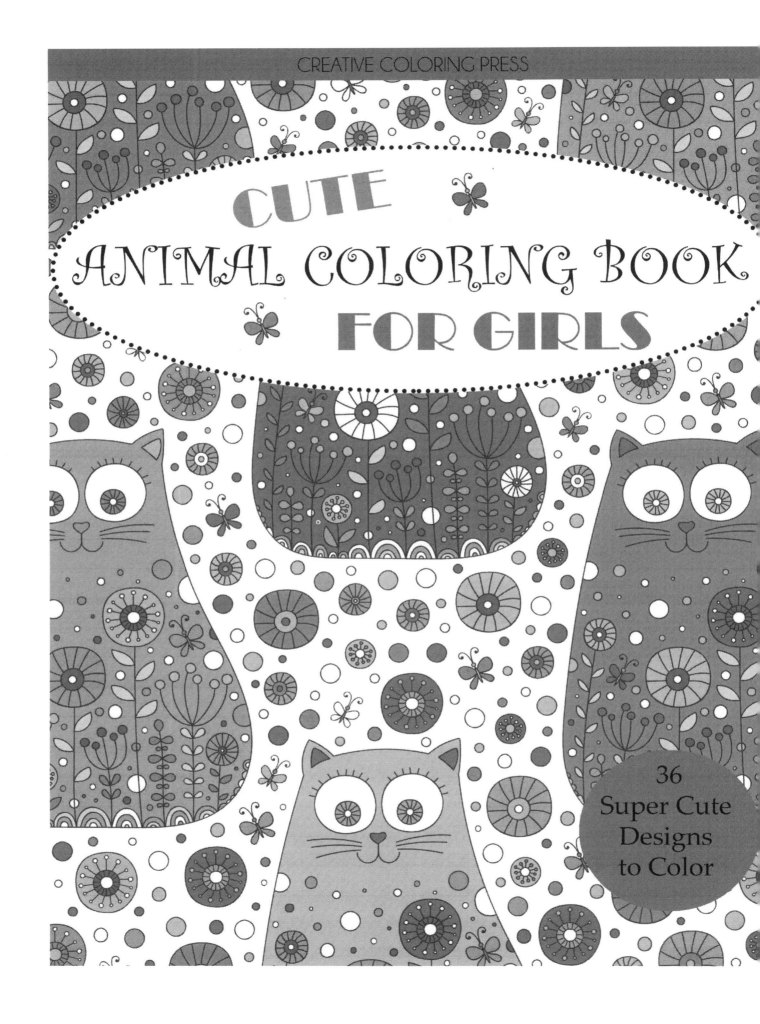

INSPIRATIONAL
COLORING BOOKFOR GIRLS

LOVE THIS LIFE

30 INSPIRING QUOTES TO COLOR

ALISA CALDER

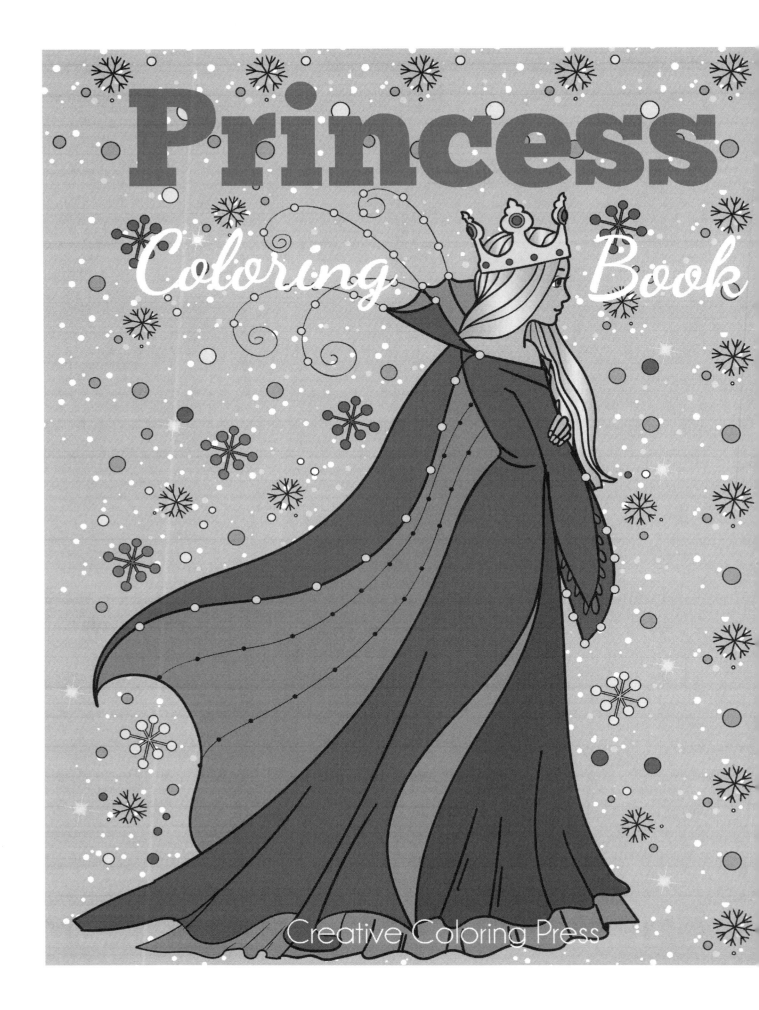

Printed in Great Britain
by Amazon